Harry Schiffer · Robert Engele

Graz

BILDER EINER STADT
PICTURES OF A CITY

styria regional

„City of Design“ – aber mit Sahnehäubchen

Ja, Graz ist mehr. Mehr als die schmückenden Bezeichnungen „Kulturhauptstadt“ (2003) oder „City of Design“ (2011) und „Weltkulturerbe“ (1999) auszusagen vermögen. Graz ist nämlich lebenswert. Und das ist viel mehr wert als alle Titel dieser Welt – denn das spüren die Menschen tagtäglich. Die, die hier leben ebenso wie die Gäste, die als Touristen die Stadt an der Mur besuchen. Schon Napoleon Bonaparte soll bei seinem (kriegerischen) Aufenthalt die steirische Hauptstadt als „la ville de Graz au bord de l´Amour“ bezeichnet haben. Das sagt einiges aus über das Lebensgefühl in Graz, auch wenn dem Korsen dabei ein sprachlicher Irrtum unterlaufen ist, denn „la Mur“ hat in Wirklichkeit wenig mit der Liebe zu tun – aber sie klingt genauso. Auf Französisch wenigstens. Sein und Schein im Grazer Alltag eben, aber immer mit dem Mehrwert eines Sahnehäubchens, zu dem man hier jedoch „Schlag“ sagt. Und darauf bestehen wir. Das hier so heimische Gefühl aus südlicher Lebensfreude und Leichtigkeit vermischt mit mitteleuropäischem Arbeitseifer und Ernst spiegelt sich nicht nur in der Architektur wider, sondern auch in den vielen Schanigärten und Straßencafés, die sich während der warmen Jahreszeit in der ganzen Stadt ausbreiten und voller Leben sind. Und es spiegelt sich in vielen Bewohnern – auch wenn manche lieber ihren Grant pflegen. Dennoch: Eine Leichtigkeit des Seins schwebt über der ganzen Stadt vom Hauptplatz, quer durch die engen Gassen der Altstadt bis zum Stadtpark und weiter zu den Universitäten. Man muss nur ihre Spur aufnehmen und ihr folgen. Denn Graz ist eine Stadt zum Spazieren und Flanieren. Hinter jeder Ecke, hinter kleinen Durchgängen und Portalen öffnet sich eine neue kleine Welt und zeigt Idyllen, romantische Gärten, historische Innenhöfe oder auch nur Sammelstellen für Mistkübel. Aber auch echte Höhepunkte gibt es dabei zu entdecken: Im Hotel Erzherzog Johann ein prachtvoller Wintergarten, im Kaufhaus Kastner & Öhler eine fünf Stockwerke hohe Jugendstilhalle oder im Gasthaus Krebsenkeller, da öffnet sich ein schmaler, langer Durchgang zum unvergleichlichen Gastgarten im Renaissancehof. Der Besucher muss nur seiner Neugierde freien Lauf lassen, in die kleinen Gassen gehen und hinter die Kulissen schauen. Es zahlt sich aus.

Auf keinen Fall versäumen sollte man einen Besuch des Schloßbergs, in dessen Schutz sich im 12. Jahrhun-

dert langsam die Stadt entwickelt hat. Die Aussicht von oben auf die rote Dachlandschaft der Altstadt ist überragend. Aber auch der Glockenturm Liesl, der Uhrturm, die Kasematten mit ihrer Freiluftbühne, der Türkenbrunnen, die Parkanlagen und alten Basteien sind einen Rundgang wert. Sollte jemand müde sein, laden viele Sitzbänke zum Rasten ein – ebenso wie die zahlreichen Kaffeehäuser mit ihren Gastgärten.

Wo der Schloßberg in den Stadtpark übergeht, entstand im 16. Jahrhundert die imperiale Stadtkrone von Graz, die aus Alter Universität, Schauspielhaus, Jesuitenkolleg, Dom mit dem Mausoleum von Kaiser Ferdinand II. und Burg mit der spätgotischen Doppelwendeltreppe von Kaiser Maximilian I. besteht. Von hier regierten die habsburgischen Herrscher ganz Innerösterreich, also Steiermark, Kärnten, Krain, Görz, Triest und Teile Istriens. Von hier gelangt man aber auch durch das Burgtor in den Stadtpark. Dort wird die andere Seite von Graz sichtbar: Die aufmüpfige, moderne Welt der revolutionären Jungen. Vom Forum Stadtpark zogen in den 1960er Jahren die jungen wilden Literaten Peter Handke, Wolfgang Bauer und Alfred Kolleritsch aus und machten Graz zur „heimlichen Hauptstadt der deutschsprachigen Literatur". Seit 1968 provozierte lange Jahre der „steirische herbst" als Avantgarde-Festival das bürgerliche Graz, heute ist auch er etabliert. Ja, Graz lag immer schon am Schnittpunkt vieler Gegensätze – Kleinstadt im Grünen und moderne Großstadt, verträumte Pensionopolis der k.u.k. Beamten ebenso wie pulsierende Universitätsstadt, nationale „Stadt der Volkserhebung" und grün-alternative Probebühne der Politik.

Heute spielt sich das junge, künstlerische und gesellige Leben eher im Lendviertel um Kunsthaus und Acconci-Murinsel ab, im Univiertel oder im sogenannten Bermuda-Dreieck um Mehlplatz, Schubertkino und Glockenspielplatz, wo schon so mancher Gast einfach verschwunden ist – denn hier reiht sich gefährlich Lokal an Lokal, die alle von Frühjahr bis Herbst ihre einladenden Gastgärten vor den Häusern aufgebaut haben. Sollte aber jemandem nach mehr Ruhe zumute sein, setzt man sich einfach in eine der weitläufigen Parkanlagen oder in eines der vielen Kaffeehäuser, liest eine Zeitung, genießt eine Melange, beobachtet zwischendurch die Menschen und – ganz langsam, allmählich, fühlt man den Pulsschlag dieser Stadt.

'City of Design' – but with a whipped cream of topping

Yes, Graz is a touch more. Much more than the decorative honorifics 'Capital of Culture' (2003) or 'City of Design' (2011) and 'World Heritage' (1999) can convey. The reason: Graz is simply worthwhile living in. This means far more than all the titles in the world - it is something people feel day in and day out. That is to say those who live here as well as the guests that come to visit this City on the River Mur. Even Napoleon Bonaparte, during his (albeit bellicose) sojourn, is said to have called Styria's capital 'la ville de Graz au bord de l'Amour'. Even though the Corsican committed a linguistic mistake, 'La Mur' having little in common with 'l'amour' - though they sound alike, such a statement certainly says much about the attitude towards life in Graz. At least in French. Nevertheless, this is the appearance and reality of daily life in Graz, but always with a whipped cream topping, which we call 'Schlag'. Of this, we are convinced.

The homely feeling of the southern love of life and lightness blended with the Central European zeal for work and commitment is not only reflected in the architecture but also in the many bustling outdoor restaurants and street cafés that can be found all over town during the warm season. It is also reflected in the attitude of many of the town's inhabitants - even though some of them prefer to wallow in their proverbial grumpiness. Nevertheless: a certain lightness of being floats over the whole city, from the main square, right through the narrow lanes of the old town, to the City Park and on to its universities. You only have to find the traces and then follow them, because Graz is a town to walk and stroll in. Around every corner, at the end of small passages and portals quaint new worlds open up in the form of idyllic spots, romantic gardens, historic inner courtyards or sometimes collections of wheelie-bins. But there are also true highlights to discover: the splendid conservatory in the Hotel Erzherzog Johann, the five-storied art nouveau hall in the Kastner & Öhler department store or the incomparable renaissance courtyard of Restaurant Krebsenkeller which can be reached through a long, narrow passageway. Visitors only have to give their curiosity free rein, step into the narrow lanes and look behind the scenes. It is really worthwhile.

Under no circumstances should you miss visiting the Schloßberg under which the city gradually developed in the 12th century. The view from above, over the old town's red roofscape is simply superb. As are the bell tower, called 'Liesl', the clock tower, the casemates with their open air stage, the Turks' well, the parks and old bastions which are all worth exploring. When you are tired, numerous benches invite you to sit down, as do the many cafés with their outdoor gardens. In the area where the Schloßberg merges with the City Park, the imperial 'City Crown' of Graz developed in the 16th century, consisting of the Old University, the Theatre, the Jesuit College, the Cathedral with the Emperor Ferdinand II Mausoleum, and the Burg (castle) with its double spiral staircase built by Emperor Maximilan I. From here, the Habsburg rulers ruled over the whole of Inner Austria, i.e. Styria, Carinthia, Carniola, Gorizia, Trieste and parts of Istria. On walking through the Burg-Gate, you reach the City Park, where you can see an entirely different face of Graz: the controversial, modern world of revolutionary youth. In the 1960s, the young, wild writers Peter Handke, Wolfgang Bauer and Alfred Kolleritsch set out from Forum Stadtpark and made Graz the 'secret capital of German literature'. From 1968 onwards, the avant-garde festival 'steirischer herbst' (Styrian autumn) has provoked bourgeois Graz, but has now become part of the establishment. Yes, Graz has always been the crossroads of many contrasts - a small town in the countryside and a modern city, a dreamy town for retired imperial officials and a pulsating university town, the national 'City of Popular Uprising' and the green-alternative stage for politics.

Today, young people and artists gather for informal get-togethers in the Lend Quarter, around the Kunsthaus and the Acconci Island in the River Mur, in the University Quarter or in the so-called 'Bermuda Triangle' around Mehlplatz, the Schubert Cinema and Glockenspielplatz, where many a guest is said to have disappeared forever in the numerous pubs and inns that offer inviting outside drinking and dining on their doorsteps from spring to autumn. However, if your mood longs for something more tranquil, simply go and relax in one of the spacious parks or in one of the many cafés, read a newspaper, enjoy a cappuccino, watch people and very leisurely feel the pulse of the city.

Wenn Sie mehr über Graz erfahren wollen, laden wir Sie nun ein, die folgende „Stadtrundfahrt" mitzuerleben, die eine etwas andere Art der Stadtführung darstellt …

Eine ganz besondere Stadtrundfahrt

Diskret räuspert sich Erzherzog Johann[1] und wischt den Schweiß von seiner hohen Stirn. Die Sonne scheint heiß auf Graz, und überdies zwickt ihn der graue Rock um die Mitte. Anscheinend hat er schon wieder zugenommen. Und überhaupt – wo bleiben heute die Gäste?

Etwas verärgert dreht er sich zu Peter Rosegger[2] um. „Wann geht's endlich los, Peter?" Doch der greift nur nervös an seine schmale Brille, tippt ein SMS weiter und murmelt: „Frag doch den Wolfi." Aber Wolfgang Bauer, einst Schrecken der Grazer Literaturszene, glänzt durch Abwesenheit. Geistig wenigstens. Körperlich sitzt auch er im Bus – ein fast perfekter Doppelgänger des trinkfreudigen Literaten, der geduldig mit den anderen sechs historischen Größen der steirischen Kulturszene auf 15 Uhr wartet. Ja, Erzherzog Johann, Peter Rosegger, Wolfgang Bauer[3], Robert Stolz[4], Arnold Schwarzenegger[5], Johannes Kepler[6] und Katharina Prato[7] oder, falls sie ausfällt, Steffi Werger[8] beziehungsweise ihre Doppelgänger, sollen Graz ins Rampenlicht setzen. Und zwar pünktlich um 15 Uhr, denn da beginnt jeden Sonntag und jeden Mittwoch im offenen Autobus die „Kulturelle Überraschungsfahrt" oder auch „Surprise Tour" durch Graz. Und sie sind die Überraschungen der Fahrt – sieben Persönlichkeiten aus Geschichte, Kultur und Wissenschaft, die quer durch die Jahrhunderte in Graz gelebt und gewirkt haben.

In Wirklichkeit stellen sie aber nicht nur die Überraschung für die Gäste dar, nein, sie sind vielmehr der Hit des gesamten Stadttourismusprogramms, um sie reißen sich die Gäste und wollen persönlich erleben, worüber sie staunend in Magazinen und Zeitungen gelesen haben – eine Besichtigungsfahrt der anderen Art, bei der historische Persönlichkeiten selbst aus ihrer Zeit erzählen. Voller Witz und mit charmanten Anekdoten. Zwanglos nehmen die Doppelgänger auf den Sitzen des Busses Platz, direkt neben den Fahrgästen. Ihre Aufgabe ist, bloß nicht aus der Rolle zu fallen, die sie spielen. Und die Gäste zu unterhalten. So hat der Erzherzog beispielsweise jovial näselnd aus seiner Epoche zu erzählen – wie Napoleon Bonapartes Truppen 1809 Graz eingenommen, aber vergebens den Schloßberg belagert haben. Oder – besonders beliebt beim Publikum – wie er die Postmeisterstochter Anna Plochl kennen und lieben gelernt hat. Oder schon etwas politischer, wie der „steirische Prinz", auch der „grüne Rebell" genannt, 1848 in Frankfurt zum deutschen Reichsverweser gewählt wurde. Ja, da sind schon viele schöne Geschichten zu erzählen. Und wenn sie aus dem Mund der Person kommen, die sie selbst erlebt hat, ist das etwas ganz Besonderes.

Die mitfahrende Fremdenführerin spielt die Rolle der Moderatorin. Immer wieder stellt sie den Sieben neue Fragen, vor allem dann, wenn sie merkt, dass diese den Faden der Handlung verloren haben. Wolfi Bauer beispielsweise deckt den Part der modernen Literatur und Szenekultur ab. Sozusagen die Zeit, in der Graz die „heimliche Literaturhauptstadt der deutschen Sprache" genannt wurde – damals in den späten 60er und 70er Jahren des 20. Jahrhunderts. Da fallen Namen wie Gerhard Roth, Peter Handke, Alfred Kolleritsch, da kommt Herwig von Kreuzbruck ebenso zu Ehren wie Gunter Falk, Barbara Frischmuth oder Reinhard P. Gruber, die „Manuskripte" nicht zu vergessen. Literarische Anekdoten und kurze Leseproben aus den Werken der Poeten berieseln die Gäste. Das ist Literatur live. Ganz nebenbei macht er wie selbstverständlich auch gleich den Gasthausführer und preist die besten Trinklokale der Stadt an, wenn sie daran vorbeifahren. Schließlich gilt er als wahrer Kenner dieser Szene.

„Meine Damen und Herren, nehmen Sie bitte Platz. In zwei Minuten fahren wir ab", schallt es nun endlich aus dem Lautsprecher. Direkt neben dem neobarocken Prachtbau des Opernhauses steht der Kabriobus im Schatten des weitläufigen Stadtparks, der Motor startet, der Bus füllt sich.

Nun also geht es los. Etwa ein Dutzend in- und ausländische Gäste nehmen an der Fahrt teil. „Coca Cola haben", quängelt die etwas schrille Stimme eines kleinen Buben in die begrüßenden Worte der Fremdenführerin. Ja, auch eine steirische Familie aus Leibnitz ist mit ihrem Kind an Bord. Es ist wirklich heiß und der kühlende Fahrtwind daher eine wahre Wohltat an diesem Sommertag. Langsam fährt der Bus die breite Allee des Opernrings entlang nach Westen. Auf den breiten Gehsteigen flanieren hübsche Mädchen in aufregenden Miniröcken, während links die alte Thalia samt Café und Sonnenschirmen zu sehen ist, rechts das Operncafé mit Gastgarten, die Kellner eilen schwitzend zu den Tischen und servieren Kaffee und kühle Drinks. Doch schon weist die Fremdenführerin rechts auf den Platz am Eisernen Tor, hinter dem sich der Blick auf die Herrengasse öffnet, die mit bunten Fahnen geschmückt ist. Die Fremdenführerin schwärmt vom Zeughaus mit seiner einmaligen Sammlung alter Waffen, vom Landhaus mit dem wunderschönen Renaissance-Innenhof und den vielen Straßencafés, die das südliche Flair der Stadt ausmachen. „Hier lässt es sich leben", nickt ein Gast zufrieden und streicht über seinen mächtigen Bauch. Der Bus fährt weiter bis zur Neutorgasse, biegt rechts ab, rollt am Gasthaus „Gösser" vorbei, bei dessen Anblick Wolfi Bauer zustimmend rülpst, biegt links ab und hält in der Kaiserfeldgasse 25, direkt neben dem Hintereingang der „Gösser".

Jetzt ist Peter Rosegger an der Reihe. Denn an dieser Stelle befand sich hier einst die Handelsakademie, die der junge Mann vom Lande von 1865 bis 1869 besucht hat, bevor er zum steirischen Nationalpoeten wurde. Ja, Peter erzählt gerne, wie es früher einmal war in der rauen Bergwelt der Waldheimat, als er noch der kleine Waldbauernbub war. Wie er als Kind zum ersten Mal mit der Eisenbahn gefahren ist, die damals noch „Dampfwagen" genannt wurde und wie er nach Mariazell wanderte. Ganz ernst wird Rosegger aber immer, wenn er vom Jahr 1913 erzählt, als er fast den Literaturnobelpreis erhalten hat. Aber eben nur fast. „Ums Arschlecken", pflegt Rosegger dann zu erzählen, hat er es nicht geschafft. Und das „A" im „Arschlecken" zelebriert Roseggers Doppelgänger besonders gedehnt mit einem Hauch von „O", echt steirisch halt.

Den Preis hat der bengalische Literat und Philosoph Rabindranath Tagore (heute Thakur genannt) überreicht bekommen. International war Roseggers Nähe zur deutschnationalen Agitation nicht ganz so gut angekommen. Er hat nämlich deutsche Schulen in den gemischtsprachigen Gebieten von Böhmen und Mähren gefördert. „Eine Schutzsammlung habe ich gemacht, um an den bedrohten Sprachgrenzen deutschen Kindern deutsche Schulen zu bauen oder zu erhalten, unter dem Leitwort: Uns zum Schutz, niemandem zum Trutz! ... Wir wehren uns um Schillers Sprache, um Goethes Kultur. Wenn mir deshalb der

Nobelpreis verloren ging, dann wohl mir", zitiert er sich selbst aus einem seiner Briefe.

Der Bus gibt Gas und fährt um das mächtige Gebäude der alten Hauptpost herum direkt ins nahe Joanneum-Museumsviertel. Die Besucher blicken nach links, und die Fremdenführerin erzählt vom großen Umbau des Museumsquartiers zum Gedenkjahr für Erzherzog Johann 1811/2011, wobei das Naturkundemuseum erst im März 2013 eröffnet wurde. Dabei wischt sich Johann den Schweiß von der Stirn und nickt zustimmend, er schwitzt wirklich sehr leicht. Verschieden große Glastrichter sind in den Innenhof gebaut, die Licht in die Museumstrakte werfen. Im größten dieser Trichter können die Besucher auf einer Rolltreppe in den Eingangsbereich der Museen und der Landesbibliothek hinunterfahren. Als letzte Erinnerung an den alten botanischen Garten des steirischen Prinzen stehen zwischen den Glastrichtern Sonnenschirme und werfen ihre Schatten auf die extravaganten Tische des Museums-Cafés. Ein Park der anderen Art eben, doch der Bus fährt schon die paar Meter zum Amtshaus weiter.

Plötzlich tönt Musik aus dem Lautsprecher des Busses. „Adieu, mein kleiner Gardeoffizier… auch du wirst mich einmal betrügen", liegt in der warmen Luft. Robert Stolz räuspert sich. „Im Haus Schmiedgasse Nummer 26, an dessen Stelle heute das Amtshaus steht, wurde ich am 25. August 1880 als zwölftes Kind meiner Eltern geboren. Ich war ein musikalisches Wunderkind und habe mit sieben Jahren schon mein erstes öffentliches Konzert gegeben. Mit 15 habe ich dann zu komponieren begonnen." Kein Wunder, könnte man sagen, bei diesen Eltern. Der Vater war Dirigent, die Mutter Pianistin. Und die Freunde der Familie hießen Johannes Brahms und Anton Bruckner, die beide die große Begabung des kleinen Robert förderten. Der war aber mehr von der leichten Musik des Johann Strauß beeindruckt und schrieb unsterbliche Schlager wie den orientalischen Foxtrott „Salome" oder das beliebte Wienerlied „Im Prater blüh'n wieder die Bäume". Am liebsten würde das Double von Robert Stolz ununterbrochen weiterreden und erzählen, dass Stolz 1930 clever den Zeitgeist erkannt hat, als der Tonfilm seinen Siegeszug antrat. Denn in diesem Jahr komponierte Stolz den ersten europäischen Musikfilm „Zwei Herzen im Dreivierteltakt". 1937 verließ er aus Protest gegen die Nazis die Heimat und zog nach Paris, wo er seine fünfte Frau, Yvonne Luise Ulrich, genannt „Einzi" („Weil sie die Einzige ist", Originalzitat) kennenlernte. Mit ihr wanderte er 1940 in die USA aus, wo er als Nobody wieder von ganz vorne beginnen musste. Schnell schaffte Stolz aber den Sprung an die Spitze. Für seine Musik in „Spring Parade" (1941) und „It Happened Tomorrow" (1944) wurde er sogar für den Oscar nominiert. Aber das denkt sich der Doppelgänger alles nur, schließlich soll er ja die Gäste unterhalten und nicht mit zu vielen Informationen quälen. Also trällert er glückselig die „Salome" und sieht den hübschen Mädchen auf der Straße nach. Sogar als Double ist er der große Frauenfreund geblieben.

Die Musik aus dem Lautsprecher übertönt langsam den singenden Doppelgänger und der Bus nimmt wieder Fahrt auf, biegt nach rechts in die Raubergasse, wo einst der Reckturm gestanden ist, in dem die Delinquenten gefoltert wurden, überquert die Kaiserfeldgasse und kommt wieder auf den Joanneumring. Und damit in den Stau. Denn Horden von schwarz-weiße Fahnen schwingenden Fußball-Fans ziehen in diesem Moment quer über den Ring nach Süden in die Liebenauer UPC-Arena, die kurze Zeit auch „Arnold-Schwarzenegger-Stadion" geheißen hat. Heute Abend spielt Sturm Graz, und da ist in der Stadt stets der Bär los. Nach einem Hupkonzert reiht sich der Bus rechts ein und fährt noch einmal durch die Neutorgasse, rechts erhascht man einen schnellen Blick auf das Joanneumsviertel, dann kommt schon das „Goldene Kalb" des Hans Hollein, das als Blickfang vor dem Museum aufgestellt ist. Weiter geht die Fahrt über den Andreas-Hofer-Platz geradeaus in den schmalen Teil der Neutorgasse. Jetzt befinden sie sich mitten in der Altstadt. Vor der Erzherzog-Johann-Brücke (vormals Hauptbrücke) bleibt der Bus stehen und gibt den Panoramablick frei auf die blaue Blase des Kunsthauses (links am anderen Murufer), auf die metallene Murinsel mitten im Fluss, die durch zwei Stege mit den Ufern verbunden ist. Beide Konstruktionen sind Erinnerungen an das Kulturhauptstadtjahr 2003, das in Graz einen touristischen Quantensprung eingeläutet hat. Rechts hingegen – wie als Kontrastprogramm – wandert der Blick in die enge Murgasse. Hier standen einst das äußere und innere Murtor und schützten die einzige Brücke über die Mur. Auch der wuchtige Unterbau der nahen Franziskanerkirche erinnert deutlich daran, dass ihr wehrhafter Turm Teil der alten Stadtmauer war.

Nun ist es höchste Zeit für den Auftritt von Johannes Kepler, der als einer der großen Begründer der modernen Naturwissenschaft gilt. Denn hier in der Murgasse, wo sich heute der Paradeishof des Großkaufhauses Kastner & Öhler befindet, stand einst die evangelische Stiftsschule, an der der 23-jährige Kepler zwischen 1594 und 1600 Mathematik unterrichtet hat. Es war damals die unruhige Zeit der Glaubenskämpfe zwischen Katholiken und Protestanten gewesen. Graz war Residenzstadt von Innerösterreich und erlebte gerade seine zweite Blütezeit, als Erzherzog Karl II. mit strenger Hand herrschte und die prächtige Stadtkrone um Karmeliterplatz, Dom und Burg ausbauen ließ. Unbeirrt von allen Agitationen der Gegenreformation begann Kepler in Graz mit der Ausarbeitung seiner Kosmologischen Theorie, die er 1597 als „Mysterium Cosmographicum" veröffentlichte. „Anno 1599 habe ich sogar den mons Sekkl, den man heute Schöckl nennt und der nun als Hausberg der Grazer bei St. Radegund gilt, bestiegen", erzählt Kepler launig, „um dem Mond näher zu sein und ihn in der klaren Bergluft besser beobachten und studieren zu können." Der ganz in Schwarz gekleidete Kepler, nur von einer weißen Halskrause aufgehellt, schildert blumig, wie er Barbara Mühleck, die Tochter eines reichen Müllers aus der näheren Umgebung von Graz, geheiratet hat und mit ihr vier Kinder bekam. Auch von seiner Wohnung in der Stempfergasse erzählt er, die sich in dem Haus befand, in dem lange Zeit der urige Keplerkeller zur Einkehr eingeladen hat. Heute ist in denselben gewölbten Räumlichkeiten ein mexikanisches Restaurant untergebracht. Zornig bebt seine Stimme immer dann, wenn er auf das Jahr 1600 zu sprechen kommt, als alle Protestanten des Landes verwiesen wurden, wenn sie sich nicht zum rechten Glauben der katholischen Kirche bekehren wollten. „Und so wanderte auch ich damals weiter nach Prag und Linz", sagt Kepler mit leiser, aber eindringlicher Stimme, setzt sich zufrieden wieder auf seinen Platz und nimmt einen guten Schluck aus seiner Trinkflasche.

Den größten Erfolg beim Reisepublikum hat aber zweifellos bei jeder Fahrt Arnold Schwarzenegger, die „Steirische Eiche" aus Thal bei Graz. Der Bodybuilder, Mr. Universum, Hollywood-Schauspieler und zweimalige Gouverneur von Kalifornien ist der Einzige, der bei diesen Busfahrten allen Gästen bekannt ist. Und wenn er sich lässig in seinem Sitz räkelt und seine Finger mit einer dicken Zigarre spielen, bleibt kein einziger Fotoapparat in der Runde still. Wenn Arnie seine romantische Bootsfahrt mit Maria Shriver über den Thalersee schildert und wie er dabei um ihre Hand angehalten hat, bleibt kein Auge trocken. Und wenn er sein berühmtes „I'll be back" oder „Hasta la vista, baby" knurrt, seufzen die Männer ebenso wie die Frauen. Arnolds Double ist nämlich ein besonders attraktiver Bodybuilder aus der Grazer Szene, der seine Armmuskeln unaufhörlich tanzen lässt. So nebenbei verteilt Arnie bei jeder Gelegenheit die Visitenkarten seines neuen Museums in Thal und macht allen weiß, dass der Weg dorthin gar nicht so weit sei. „Mamas Apfelstrudel ist wirklich der beste", murmelt er noch und hebt beide Arme zur Siegespose. Frenetischer Applaus brandet hier jedes Mal auf.

Unter diesen Bedingungen hat es die einzige Frau in der erlesenen Runde natürlich bedeutend schwerer. Katharina Prato ist ihr Name und sie hat 1858 das berühmteste Kochbuch der Donaumonarchie geschrieben, „Die süddeutsche Küche". Damit hat sie einen Bestseller sondergleichen gelandet, der bis heute immer wieder nachgedruckt wird.[9] Doch berühmt ist sie heute nicht mehr. „Der eigentliche Entstehungsgrund für mein Kochbuch war das Magenleiden meines Mannes Eduard Pratobevera, von seinen Freunden kurz ‚Prato' gerufen", erzählt die dunkelhaarige Schönheit. „Er war Professor für Weltgeschichte in Wien, nach seiner krankheitsbedingten Pensionierung ist er aber nach Graz gezogen, ins Pensionopolis der Monarchie, wo er ein junges Mädchen kennen- und lieben lernte – mich", fügt sie stolz hinzu. „Als seine Frau musste ich mir stets neue Speisen ausdenken, die er vertragen hat." Und Freunde ermunterten sie, aus den vielen Rezepten doch ein Buch zu machen. Also nahm sie als Buchautorin den Spitznamen ihres Mannes an. Pratos Spezialität war, dass sie stets am Puls ihrer Zeit war und alle Neuerungen sofort in die neueste Auflage ihres Buches aufnahm. „Sie müssen sich das aus dem Zeitgeist heraus vorstellen", erklärt sie den Gästen. „Damals kam die kleine bürgerliche Familie auf, die sich eine Köchin nicht mehr leisten konnte. Da musste die Bürgersfrau selbst kochen – hatte das aber nie richtig gelernt und war auch nicht auf die Bewirtung von Gästen vorbereitet. Also habe ich für alles, was eine junge Frau können musste, ein Kapitel geschrieben und bei jeder Neuauflage stets die aktuellen Neuerungen der großen weiten Welt eingebaut. Da gab es ein Kapitel über das ‚Moderne Servieren', dann über die ‚Gesetze der Chemie' und die ‚Gesundheitslehre'. Als 1876 das metrische System in Österreich-Ungarn eingeführt wurde, habe ich natürlich sofort einen Anhang über ‚Berechnungen nach dem metrischen Maß und Gewicht' eingefügt. Als der englische Fünfuhrtee im Salon in Mode kam, habe ich ihm sogleich ein eigenes Kapitel gewidmet", lächelt sie. „Mich freut, dass meine typische Redewendung ‚Man nehme ...', mit der ich viele Rezepte in meinem Buch beginne, heute noch gebräuchlich ist." Was sie noch freut, erklärt dann die Fremdenführerin: Seit Kurzem gibt es im Palais Herberstein in der Sackstraße sogar ein Restaurant, das Pratos Namen trägt. Dass die meisten Gäste Frau Prato nicht kennen, steckt diese mit Charme und ihrem attraktiven Aussehen locker weg. Ihr besonderer Pluspunkt, der für viel Sympathie sorgt: Sie verteilt großzügig köstliche Pralinen, während sie landestypische Rezepte erklärt, dass einem das Wasser im Mund zusammenläuft.

Wenn das Prato-Double keine Zeit für die Überraschungsfahrten hat, weil sie nebenbei auch als Model arbeitet, springt gerne die Doppelgängerin von Steffi Werger ein. Die Sängerin, Texterin, Kabarettistin und Buchautorin mit der unverwechselbaren Stimme beginnt ihre Show immer auf dieselbe Art. „Legenden sterben nicht im Bett", flüstert sie heiser ins Mikro und plaudert über die Grazer Kabarettszene. Sie erzählt vom legendären Theatercafé in der Mandellstraße gleich hinter dem Opernhaus, vom Orpheum und den anderen Bühnen der Kleinkunstszene. Ihre Stimme ist stark wie ein Felsen, wenn sie von den Höhen und Tiefen einer österreichischen Popsängerin mit Niveau spricht. Und von den Gefahren, die im Popgeschäft lauern. Denn sie kennt vieles aus persönlicher Erfahrung. „Aber das einzige weiße Pulver, das mir zum Verhängnis wurde, ist der Zucker", lacht sie. „In Wahrheit kannst du dir als österreichische Sängerin über 20, die eventuell noch im Dialekt singt, gleich die Kugel geben", hat Steffi einmal in einem Interview erklärt. Schade eigentlich, dass sie nicht öfter im Bus mitfährt, denn ihre Erzählungen sprechen vor allem das jüngere Publikum an, ihre Lieder sind großartig – und Kabarett kommt bei den Gästen immer gut an.

Während die Sonne heiß in den Kabriobus scheint und die Gäste fast schon ein Wett-Trinken veranstalten, ist das Fahrzeug bereits auf dem Weg zum Schloss Eggenberg. Dort sollen die Gäste nicht nur das schöne Barockschloss besichtigen, sondern auch in das Geheimnis der berühmten Zahlenmystik eingeweiht werden, nach der es gebaut wurde. Die gesamte Architektur entspricht ja der strengen Zahlenallegorie des 1583 bei uns neu eingeführten Gregorianischen Kalenders. Den 365 Jahrestagen entspricht die Zahl der Außenfenster, jedes Stockwerk enthält 31 Räume, die vier Ecktürme stellen die vier Jahreszeiten dar, 24 Prunkräume entsprechen den 24 Stunden und so weiter und so fort. Doch die Tour geht auch nach Schloss Eggenberg, damit sich die Gäste in den prächtigen Parkanlagen ein wenig von den Strapazen des Tages erholen können. Denn zugegeben, es ist eine wirklich sehr intensive Fahrt mit vielen neuen Eindrücken und Showelementen, aber ein Erlebnis der Sonderklasse, das jeden Teilnehmer begeistert. „Dafür zahle ich gerne etwas mehr", freut sich der Gast mit dem großen Bauch und lacht zufrieden.

Der Bus fährt nun langsam durch die schattige Eggenberger Allee und der Schlosspark ist bereits zu sehen, als sich die Musik plötzlich ändert und immer lauter wird. Das ist doch, ja wirklich – es ist der Erzherzog-Johann-Jodler, der jetzt aus dem Lautsprecher ertönt – aber als Rap-Song eigenwillig interpretiert. „Willkommen in Graz", sagt die Fremdenführerin und steht auf.

1 Erzherzog Johann von Österreich (* 1782 in Florenz, † 1859 in Graz), Bruder von Kaiser Franz I., wurde als der „steirische Prinz" bezeichnet, weil er ein halbes Jahrhundert lang der Förderer und Modernisierer der steirischen Industrie, Wirtschaft und Wissenschaft war. Heiratete die Postmeisterstochter Anna Plochl, was der Kaiser lange zu verhindern versuchte, wurde 1848 deutscher Reichsverweser.

2 Peter Rosegger (* 1843 in Alpl, † 1918 in Krieglach), Sohn eines armen Waldbauern, wurde Wanderschneider, begann zu schreiben, übersiedelte nach Graz und wurde der bekannteste steirische Volksdichter, vor allem die Erzählungen „Waldheimat" (1874) aus seiner Jugend sind sehr authentisch und beliebt. Hätte 1913 fast den Literaturnobelpreis erhalten, was aber aus politischen Gründen verhindert wurde.

3 Wolfgang Bauer (* 1941 in Graz, † 2005 in Graz), österreichischer Schriftsteller, der vor allem als Dramatiker international bekannt wurde. Vertreter der schriftstellerischen Avantgarde und des absurden Theaters. Durchbruch mit „Magic Afternoon" 1968, das in Hannover seine Uraufführung hatte, nachdem es von 40 Bühnen und Verlagen abgelehnt worden war. „Change" (1969). Bauer verstand sein Leben als exzessives, aktionistisches Kunstwerk.

4 Robert Stolz (* 1880 in Graz, † 1975 in Berlin), österreichischer Komponist und Dirigent, schrieb mehr als 60 Operetten sowie zahlreiche Filmmusiken, gilt als der letzte Meister der Wiener Operette. Wurde zwei Mal für den Filmmusik-Oscar nominiert.

5 Arnold Schwarzenegger (* 1947 in Thal bei Graz, lebt in Kalifornien), besuchte in Graz die Hauptschule, absolvierte hier seinen Militärdienst. Wurde weltweit erfolgreichster Bodybuilder, wanderte 1968 in die USA aus, Mr. Universum, erwirtschaftete sich in den 1970er Jahren als Immobilienmakler ein Millionenvermögen, schloss sein Studium der internationalen Wirtschaftslehre an der University of Wisconsin-Superior mit dem Bachelor of Arts ab. Wurde Hollywood-Filmschauspieler der Welterfolge „Terminator" 1, 2 und 3, „Total Recall", „Twins", „Kindergarden Cop", „True Lies", 1986 heiratete der republikanische Politiker Schwarzenegger Maria Shriver, die Nichte des Demokraten John F. Kennedy, war von 2003 bis 2011 Gouverneur von Kalifornien.

6 Johannes Kepler (* 1571 in Weil der Stadt, † 1630 in Regensburg), deutscher Naturphilosoph, Mathematiker, Astronom, Astrologe, Optiker und evangelischer Theologe, der von 1594 bis 1600 an der evangelischen Stiftsschule in Graz unterrichtete.

7 Katharina Prato (* 1818 in Graz als Katharina Polt, † 1897 in Graz), war das Pseudonym der erfolgreichen österreichischen Kochbuchautorin Katharina Pratobevera, deren Hauptwerk „Die Süddeutsche Küche" bis heute aufgelegt wird. Engagierte sich sozial als Gründerin des Vereins „Volksküche" und im Verein „Frauenheim", gründete eine Mädchenarbeitsschule und mehrere Kindergärten.

8 Stefanie Werger (* 1951 in Maria Lankowitz, lebt in Graz), österreichische Musikerin, Sängerin, Buchautorin und Kabarettistin. 2003 gewann sie den „Amadeus Austrian Music Award" in der Kategorie „Beste Künstlerin Rock/Pop national".

9 Prato, Die gute alte Küche. Neu ediert und herausgegeben von Christoph Wagner. Pichler Verlag 2006. ISBN 978-3-85431-426-4

If you would like to learn more about Graz, we invite you to experience the following 'City Tour' which is actually a tour of a different kind ...

A Very Special City Tour

Archduke Johann[1] discretely clears his throat and wipes the sweat from his high forehead. The sun burns down on Graz and, moreover, his grey coat is a little tight around his waist. It seems, he has gained weight again. And anyway - where are all the guests today?

Slightly irritated, he turns to Peter Rosegger[2]. "When does it finally start, Peter?", Peter is fumbling nervously with his glasses, types an SMS and mumbles: "Why don't you ask Wolfi!" However, Wolfgang Bauer[3], once the 'Enfant Terrible' of Graz's literature scene, is notably absent. At least mentally. Physically, he also sits in the bus. He is an almost perfect lookalike of the continuously thirsty writer, and he patiently waits, together with six other historic figures of the Styrian culture scene for 3 p.m. to arrive. Yes, Archduke Johann, Peter Rosegger, Wolfgang Bauer, Robert Stolz[4], Arnold Schwarzenegger[5], Johannes Kepler[6] and Katharina Prato[7] or if she cannot come, Steffi Werger, or rather their lookalikes are here to put Graz in the limelight. Punctually at 3 p.m., the time when every Sunday and every Wednesday a 'Cultural Surprise Tour' starts through Graz in an open bus. And they are the 'surprises' of this tour. Seven personalities from history, culture and the sciences who, in turn, have lived and worked in Graz through the centuries.

Actually, they are not only the surprise for the guests, no, they are more the hit of the entire City Tourism Programme; the guests, having read about them with astonishment in magazines and newspapers, are falling over themselves to experience them personally - a sightseeing trip of a different kind, during which the historic personalities themselves talk about their times with humour and charming anecdotes. The lookalikes casually take their seats in the bus right next to the passengers. Their task is simply not to step out of the role they play and to entertain the guests. The archduke, for instance, talks about his epoch in a jovial, nasal voice, about how Napoleon Bonaparte's forces occupied Graz in 1809 but unsuccessfully besieged Schloßberg. Or, what the audience particularly likes, how he met and fell in love with Anna Plochl, the postmaster's daughter. Or, slightly more on the political side, how the 'Styrian Prince', also called the 'Green Rebel', was elected German Regent in Frankfurt in 1848. Yes, there are many wonderful stories to tell. And when they are told by the person who actually experienced them, it makes it even more special.

The accompanying tourist guide acts as a moderator. She continuously asks the seven celebrities new questions, especially when she sees that they have gone off track. Wolfi Bauer, for example, covers the part of modern literature and scene culture. In other words, the time in which Graz was called the 'secret literature capital of the German language', back in the late 60s and 70s of the 20th century. Names such as Gerhard Roth, Peter Handke, Alfred Kolleritsch are mentioned, but also Herwig von Kreuzbruck as well as Gunter Falk, Barbara Frischmuth or Reinhard P. Gruber have their place of honour, not forgetting the magazine 'Manuskripte'. The guests are showered with anecdotes from literature and short excerpts from works of the poets. This is live literature. And as a side-line, he quite naturally acts as restaurant guide and praises the best 'watering holes' of the town as they drive by. Ultimately, he is well-known as a true connoisseur of the scene.

"Ladies and gentlemen, please take your seats. We are leaving in two minutes", the announcement finally comes over the loudspeaker. The cabrio-bus is parked in the shade of the spacious City Park, directly next to the magnificent, neo-baroque building of the Opera House; the engine starts, the bus slowly fills up.

Finally, the bus moves off. Around a dozen local and foreign guests have joined the tour. "I want a Coke", the rather shrill voice of a boy breaks into the tour guide's welcome speech. Yes, a Styrian family from Leibniz is also on board with their child. It is really stifling and the cool flowing air is greatly welcome on this hot summer day. The bus moves leisurely along the wide tree-flanked avenue, the Opernring. Pretty girls in tempting miniskirts walk along the spacious sidewalks; to the left, you can see the old Thalia with its café and sunshades; to the right, the Operncafé with outdoor seating where waiters run sweating from table to table and serve coffee and cold drinks. Then the guide indicates the Platz am Eisernen Tor to the right, where the view opens into Herrengasse which is lined with multi-coloured banners. The guide talks enthusiastically about the Zeughaus (armoury) and its unique collection of old weapons, the Landhaus with its marvellous inner courtyard from the Renaissance period and the many street cafés that instil the town with southern flair. "Here you can enjoy life", a guest nods contentedly and strokes his mighty belly. The bus continues its journey to Neutorgasse, turns right and passes the brewery restaurant 'Gösser', the sight of which makes Wolfi Bauer burp with pleasure; the bus turns left and stops at Kaiserfeldgasse 25, directly next to the rear entrance of the 'Gösser'.

Now, it is Peter Rosegger's turn, because it was here that the old Commercial School was located, which the young country boy attended from 1865 to 1869 before becoming Styrian national poet. Yes, Peter enjoys talking about how it used to be in the rough mountainous area of the Waldheimat. How, as a child, he travelled for the first time by train, which was then called 'Steam Wagon', and how he walked to Mariazell, Styria's most famous place of pilgrimage. Rosegger becomes very serious when he talks about being almost awarded the Nobel Prize for Literature in 1913. Only almost that is. In the end, the Bengali writer and philosopher Rabindranath Tagore (who today is called Thakur) received the prize. Rosegger's proximity to German nationalist agitation was not received too well. He had supported German schools in the mixed language areas of Bohemia and Moravia. "I started up a collection for the construction and maintenance of German schools for German children in the endangered language borders, under the motto: For our protection but not to spite anybody! ... We defend Schiller's language, Goethe's culture. If I was not awarded the Nobel Prize for this reason, so much the better for me", he cites from one of his own letters. The bus accelerates and drives around the impressive building of the old main post office, directly into the nearby Joanneum Museum Quarter. The visitors look to their left and the tourist guide gives an explanation about the large renovation project of the Museum Quarter for the anniversary of Archduke Johann 1811/2011. The new Natural History Museum was opened in March 2013. All the while, Johann wipes sweat from his forehead and nods approvingly; he really sweats very easily. Various large conical openings with glass surrounds are built into the inner courtyard to let light into the underground museum wings. Through the largest of these openings, visitors may use an escalator into the reception area of the museums and the provincial library. As a last memento of the old botanical garden of the Styrian prince, various sunshades stand between the conical openings and throw their shade over the extravagant tables of the museum café. A park of a different nature, but the bus is already continuing the few meters to the Amtshaus (administration building).

Suddenly music issues from the bus loudspeakers. 'Adieu, mein kleiner Gardeoffizier ... auch du wirst mich einmal betrügen (Good-bye my little soldier ... you too will once cheat on me)' floats in the air. Robert Stolz clears his throat. "I was born on 25 August 1880, the twelfth child of my parents, in the house at Schmiedgasse 26, where the Amtshaus stands today. I was a musical prodigy and gave my first public concert at the age of seven. At 15, I started composing". Not astonishingly, one could say, when one considers who his parents were. The father was a conductor, the mother a pianist. Friends of the family were Johannes Brahms and Anton Bruckner who both encouraged young Robert's outstanding talent. However, the young man was far more impressed by the light music of Johann Strauss and composed unforgettable songs such as the oriental foxtrot 'Salome' or the popular Viennese song 'Im Prater blüh'n wieder die Bäume (The trees are blossoming again in the Prater)'. Robert Stolz's lookalike would love to continue his reminiscences and explain that Stolz understood the spirit of the times of the 1930s, when the sound film started its triumphal march. It was the year, when Stolz composed the music for the first European sound movie 'Zwei Herzen im Dreivierteltakt (Two hearts in three-four time)'. In protest against the Nazis, he left his motherland in 1937 and moved to Paris, where he met his fifth wife, Yvonne Luise Ulrich, called 'Einzi' (German abbreviation of 'only') ('Because she is the only one', original quotation). He migrated to the US with her in 1940, where, being a nobody, he had to start from scratch, but he rapidly climbed to the top again. For his music in 'Spring Parade' (1941) and 'It Happened Tomorrow' (1944), he was nominated for the Academy Awards. However, his lookalike is only reflecting on this to himself; his task is to keep the guests entertained and not to torture them with too much information. So, he happily hums 'Salome' and his eyes follow the pretty girls in the street. Even as a lookalike, he continues to be a great admirer of women.

The music from the loudspeaker slowly drowns out the singing lookalike and the bus resumes its journey, turns right into Raubergasse, where once the Reckturm (a tower of the fortifications) stood in which delinquents were tortured, then crosses Kaiserfeldgasse and returns to Joanneumring, and into a traffic jam. Crowds of soccer fans brandishing black and white banners move southwards along the Ring towards the UPC Arena in Liebenau which, for a short period, was called the 'Arnold Schwarzenegger Stadium'. Tonight, the local club Sturm Graz is playing which means that all hell will break loose. After a cacophony of car horns, the bus slides into the right lane, drives once more through Neutorgasse; there is another glimpse of the Joanneum Quarter, and then the bus moves past the 'Golden Calf' that Hans Hollein has placed in front of the museum as an eye-catcher. The journey continues across Andreas-Hofer-Platz straight into the narrow section of Neutorgasse. Now, you are in the middle of the old town. The bus stops in front of Archduke Johann Bridge (previously

Hauptbrücke - Main Bridge) from where you have a panoramic view of the blue bubble of the Kunsthaus (art gallery) and the metal Mur Island in the middle of the river which is linked to both banks by two footbridges. Both constructions are mementos of the year 2003 when Graz was Capital of Culture, a year in which the city took a touristic quantum leap forward. To the right, in contrast, you get a view of the narrow Murgasse. In times past, the outer and inner Mur Gate stood here and protected the only bridge over the River Mur. The massive substructure of Franziskanerkirche (Franciscan Church) which is located close by, is a clear reminder that its defensive tower once formed part of the old city wall.

Now it is high time for Johannes Kepler, who is considered as one of the great founders of modern natural science, to play his part. Here, in Murgasse, where today the Paradeishof of the department store Kastner & Öhler is located, once stood the Protestant Monastery School where, between 1594 and 1600, 23 year old Kepler taught mathematics. It was during the uncertain times of religious conflict between Catholics and Protestants. Graz was Inner Austria's residential city and was experiencing its second heyday, when Archduke Karl II. reigned with an iron fist and had the splendid 'City Crown' around Karmeliterplatz, the Cathedral and the Castle extended. Unperturbed by the agitation of the counter-reformation, Kepler started working on his cosmological theory, which he published as 'Mysterium Cosmographicum' in 1597. "In the year 1599, I climbed 'Mons Sekkl', today called Schöckl, near St. Radegund, the local mountain of the inhabitants of Graz in order to be closer to the moon and to better observe and study it", Kepler says jokingly. Kepler, dressed completely in black with only a white ruff around his neck, explains in flowery language how he married Barbary Mühleck, the daughter of a rich miller from the vicinity of Graz, and had four children with her. He also talks about his apartment in Stempfergasse, where for a long time, the rustic Keplerkeller (a local restaurant) was open for patrons. Today, a Mexican restaurant occupies the same vaulted rooms. His voice turns angry every time he starts talking about the year 1600, when all Protestants who did not want to convert to the true faith of the Catholic church were expelled from the country. "So I travelled on to Prague and Linz", Kepler says in a low but emphatic voice, sits down again and takes a sip from his drinking bottle.

There is no doubt, however, that on each trip, the greatest success with visitors is Arnold Schwarzenegger, the 'Styrian Oak' from Thal near Graz. The body builder, Mr Universe, Hollywood actor and twice Governor of California is the only person on these bus trips, whom all guests know. When he leisurely stretches in his seat and his fingers play with a fat cigar, there is not a single camera that does not click. When Arnie tells about his romantic boat trip across Lake Thal with Maria Shriver and how he asked for her hand, tears well up in every eye. And when he growls his famous 'I'll be back' or 'Hasta la vista, baby' both the male and the female guests sigh deeply. Arnold's lookalike is a particularly attractive bodybuilder from the Graz scene, who incessantly makes the muscles of his arms dance. On the side, he distributes leaflets of his new museum near Thal and tries to make everybody believe that it is actually not too far away. "Mother's apple strudel is really the best", he mumbles and lifts both arms in a victory pose. Frenetic applause breaks out every time.

Under these conditions, the only woman in the select group of celebrities finds it infinitely difficult. Her name is Katharina Prato and she wrote the most fa-

mous cookery book of the Danube Monarchy, 'Die süddeutesche Küche (The South German Kitchen)' in 1858. It immediately became an incomparable best-seller and is still re-printed today.[9] However, she herself is no longer famous. "The actual reason for writing this cookery book was that my husband, Eduard Pratobevera, called 'Prato' by his friends, suffered from a stomach complaint", explains the dark-haired beauty. "He was professor of world history in Vienna and after retiring for medical reasons, he moved to Graz, the 'Pensionopolis' of the Monarchy, where he got to know and love a young girl, me", she adds proudly. "As his wife, I continuously had to invent new dishes his stomach could digest." Friends encouraged her to make a book out of the many recipes. As author, she used her husband's nickname. Prato's hallmark was that she stayed at the pulse of the times and included all new developments in the latest edition of her book. "You must imagine this in the context of the spirit of the times", she explains to the guests. "At that time, small, bourgeois families came into being who could not afford cooks any longer. The wife had to cook herself, however, she had never really learned it and was not prepared for catering to guests. So, I compiled everything a young woman had to know into separate chapters and whenever a new edition came out, complemented it with the latest developments of the big wide world. For instance, there was a chapter about 'Modern Serving', one about 'The Laws of Chemistry' and one about 'Advice on Health'. When, in 1876, the metric system was introduce in Austro-Hungary, I immediately added an annex on 'Calculations According to Metric Measurements and Weights'. When the English 'Five o-clock tea' became fashionable, I immediately dedicated it its own chapter", she smiles. "I am particularly happy that my typical expression 'Take ...' with which many of my recipes in the book start, is still used today." Another thing she is also happy about, is explained by the tour guide: Very recently, a restaurant has opened in Palais Herberstein in Sackgasse that bears her name. The fact that most of the guests have never heard of Ms Prato, she easily handles with charm and her attractive looks. Her big asset that generates great sympathy is: she generously distributes splendid chocolates while she explains typical local recipes that make one's mouth water.

Whenever Prato's lookalike does not have time for the surprise tours because she also works as a model, Steffi Werger's lookalike takes her place. The singer, song writer, cabaret artist and author of books has a distinctive voice and always starts her shows in the same way: "Legends do not die in bed", she throatily whispers into the microphone and starts chatting about the cabaret scene of Graz. She tells about the legendary 'Theatercafé' in Mandellstraße, just behind the Opera House, of 'Orpheum' and other cabaret stages. Her voice is as hard as steel when she speaks about the heights and depths an Austrian pop singer with class can experience. And about the dangers lurking in the pop business, as she knows many of them from experience. "However, the only white powder that became my downfall is sugar", she smiles. "In fact, if you are an Austrian singer over 20 who, in addition, sings in dialect, you may as well shoot yourself straight the head", Steffi once declared in an interview. It is a pity, she does not join the bus more often, because her stories speak mainly to the younger audience, her songs are great and cabaret is always appreciated by the guests.
While the sun keeps burning down on the cabrio-bus and the guests are almost starting a drinking competition, the bus is already on its way to Eggenberg Castle. The guests not only visit the splendid baroque castle

but are also introduced to the secret of the famous mysticism of numbers according to which it was built. The entire architecture follows the strict numeral allegory of the Gregorian calendar which was introduced in 1583. The number of windows on the outside corresponds to the 365 days of the year, each floor contains 31 rooms, the four corner towers stand for the four season, 24 staterooms represent the 24 hours etc., etc. One of the reasons the tour goes to Eggenberg Castle is to give the guests some respite from the rigours of the day and an opportunity to relax in the splendid park. Admittedly, it is a very intensive journey with many new impressions and show elements, but it is also an experience of a special category that fills all participants with enthusiasm. "I don't mind paying a little more for this," says the guest with the pronounced belly and smiles contentedly.

The bus now slowly drives along the shady Eggenberger Allee and you can see the castle park, when the music suddenly changes and gets louder and louder. Yes it is, it really is the 'Archduke Johann Yodel' that issues from the loudspeakers, interpreted, however, with the individuality of a rap song. "Welcome to Graz", the tour guide says and stands up.

1 Archduke Johann of Austria (*1782 in Florence, † 1859 in Graz), brother of Emperor Franz I, was called the 'Styrian Prince' because for over half a century, he sponsored and modernised the Styrian industry, economy and sciences. Married Anna Plochl, a postmaster's daughter; a marriage the Emperor had tried to prevent for a long time; he was nominated German Regent in1848.

2 Peter Rosegger (* 1843 in Alpl, † 1918 in Krieglach), son of a poor forester, became a tailor journeyman, started to write, moved to Graz and became the most popular folk poet; his tales about his youth in the 'Waldheimat (Home in The Forest)' (1874) in particular are very authentic and especially beloved. He was almost awarded the Nobel Prize for Literature in 1913, but it did not take place for political reasons.

3 Wolfgang Bauer (* 1941 in Graz, † 2005 in Graz), Austrian writer, mainly known internationally as a playwright. Represents the literary avant-garde and absurd theatre. His breakthrough came in 1968 with 'Magic Afternoon', which had its premiere in Hannover after having been rejected by 40 theatres and publishing houses. 'Change' (1969). Bauer saw his life as an excessive, actionist work of art.

4 Robert Stolz (* 1880 in Graz, † 1975 in Berlin), Austrian composer and director, composed over 60 operettas and numerous film scores, counts as the last master of the Viennese Operetta. He was nominated twice for the Academy Award for Best Original Score.

5 Arnold Schwarzenegger (* 1947 in Thal near Graz, lives in California), attended the General Secondary School in Graz where he also completed his military service. He became the most famous body builder worldwide, emigrated to the US in 1968, became Mr Universe, made millions as a real estate agent in the 1970s, obtained a Bachelor of Arts degree in International Economics from the University of Wisconsin-Superior. He became a Hollywood actor with worldwide hits such as 'Terminator' 1, 2 and 3, 'Total Recall', 'Twins', 'Kindergarden Cop', and 'True Lies'. In 1986, the Republican politician Schwarzenegger married Maria Shriver, niece of the Democrat John F. Kennedy, and was Governor of California from 2003 to 2011.

6 Johannes Kepler (* 1571 in Weil der Stadt, † 1630 in Regensburg), German natural philosopher, mathematician, astronomer, astrologer, optician and Protestant theologian, who taught at the Protestant Monastery School in Graz from 1594 to 1600.

7 Katharina Prato (* 1818 in Graz as Katharina Polt, † 1897 in Graz), was the pseudonym of the successful Austrian cookery author Katharina Pratobevera, whose main work 'Die Süddeutsche Küche' [The South German Kitchen] is still published today. She was socially engaged as the founder of the association 'Volksküche' [Peoples' Kitchen] and in the association 'Frauenheim' [Women's Home], founded a school for working girls and several kindergartens.

8 Stefanie Werger (* 1951 in Maria Lankowitz, lives in Graz), Austrian musician, singer, author of books and cabaret artist. Won the 'Amadeus Austrian Music Award' in the category 'Best Artist Rock/Pop National' in 2003.

9 Prato, Die gute alte Küche (The Good Old Kitchen). Newly edited and published by Christoph Wagner. Pichler Verlag 2006. ISBN 978-3-85431-426-4

Die Grazer Altstadt aus der Vogelperspektive.
The old town of Graz from a bird's eye view.

1

Blick auf Hauptplatz und Rathaus, davor das Erzherzog-Johann-Denkmal. **View of the main square and the Town Hall, with the Arch-uke Johann memorial in front.** | 2 Allegorische Flussfigur am Denkmal. **An allegorical figure of a river on the monument.**

1
GRAZ

2

3

Der Hauptplatz zur Weihnachtszeit – ein buntes Adventdorf. **The Main Square at Christmas - a colourful Advent-village.** | 2 Chor-
-eltmeisterschaft in Graz. **The World Choir Games in Graz.** | 3 Lange Tafel der Genuss-Hauptstadt. **The Long Table of the 'Capital of**
-ulinary Delights'. | 4 „Es ist noch Zeit", zeigt die Rathausuhr. **'There's still time' says the City Hall clock.** | 5 Im Flug über das Rathaus.
-flight over the City Hall.

1 Dekorative Hausfassaden in der Altstadt. **Decorative building facades in the old town.** | 2 Das Gemalte Haus war einst der alte Herzoghof. **The Painted House, also called Herzoghof.**

2
HUMANIC
pimkie

1 Alte Brunnenfigur im Landhaushof. **An old fountain sculpture in the Landhaus courtyard.** | 2 Wenn hier das „Aufsteirern" gefeiert wird, darf ein zünftiger „Schuhplattler" nicht fehlen. **When 'Aufsteirern' (Styrian fete) is celebrated, a proper 'Schuhplattler' (folk dance) is a must.** | 3 Renaissance-Arkadengang im Landhaushof. **The Renaissance arcade in the Landhaus courtyard.**

1

2

Im Zeughaus, der größten historischen Waffenkammer der Welt. **Inside the Zeughaus, the world's largest historic armoury.**
Eine Eiskrippe schmückt zur Adventzeit den Landhaushof. **A nativity scene made of ice adorns the Landhaus courtyard during Advent.**
Blick vom Landhaushof auf den Schloßberg. **A view from the Landhaus courtyard towards Schloßberg.**

1

2

Uhr am Kirchturm der Stadtpfarrkirche. The clock on the church steeple of Stadtpfarrkirche (the main parish church).
Ein Glasfenster in der Stadtpfarrkirche zeigt auch Hitler und Mussolini. A glass window in Stadtpfarrkirche includes Hitler and ussolini. | 3 Die Herrengasse öffnet sich zum Platz am Eisernen Tor. Herrengasse opens into the Platz am Eisernen Tor.

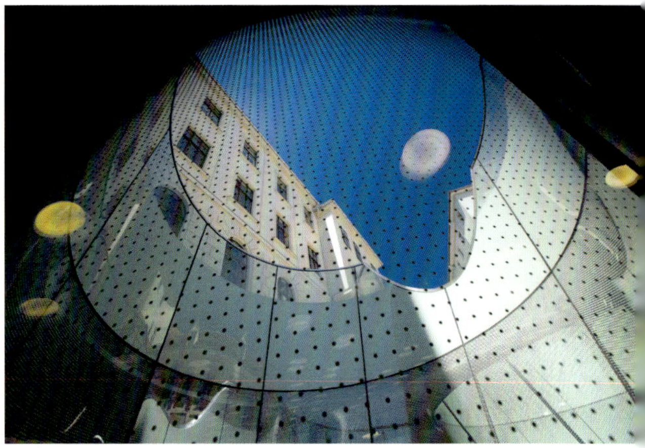

Das neue Joanneum Museumsviertel in der Altstadt: Glastrichter bringen Licht in die unterirdischen Räume und eine Rolltreppe führt di Besucher in die Unterwelt der Museen und Bücher. **The new Joanneum Museum Quarter in the old town: conical openings with glass surrounds allow light into the subterranean hall and an escalator transports visitors into the 'underworld' of the museums and boo**

Bubble & Co

1 Eine Aktion von La Strada. **A La Strada event.** | 2 Jakominiplatz – die Verkehrsdrehscheibe der Stadt. **Jakominiplatz - the city's traffic hub.** | Ein Bummel durch die Grazer Gassen. 3 Herrengasse. 4 Schmiedgassse. **A stroll through the alleys of Graz. 3 Herrengasse. 4 Schmiedgasse.**

3
HUMANIC
HUMANIC
CAFE MUHR
TEMMEL das EIS in Graz
BONITA

4

Die roten Dächer der Altstadt sind Teil des Weltkulturerbes.
The red roofs of the old town are part of the World Cultural Heritage.

1 Blick von der Franziskanerkirche zum Kunsthaus. A view from Franziskanerkirche to the Kunsthaus. | 2, 3, 4 Von Lokal zu Lokal im Kälbernen Viertel. From pub to pub in the Kälberne Viertel (a part of the old town). | 5 Ein Moment der Ruhe im Klosterhof der Franziskaner. A moment of tranquillity in the courtyard of the Franciscan Abbey.

3

1

Franziskanerkirche „Mariä Himmelfahrt" an der „bemalten" Murpromenade. **Franciscan church Maria Himmelfahrt on the "painted" Mur-omenade.** | 2 Schloßberg-Feuerwerk zu Silvester. **Fireworks on Schloßberg on New Year's Eve.** | 3 Nächtliche Idylle in der Franziska-rgasse. **Night idyll in Franziskanergasse.**

stadtmuseumgraz

KUNST

Blick vom Schloßberg. A view from Schloßberg. | 2, 3 Dekorative Kunstzeichen. Decorative art signs. | 4 Detail am Portal der riahilferkirche. A detail on the facade of Mariahilferkirche. | 5 Zunftzeichen. A guild sign. | 6 Schwebende Schirme von La Strada. ating umbrellas by La Strada. | 7 Blick von der Dreifaltigkeitskirche auf das Kunsthaus. View of the Kunsthaus from the ly Trinity Church.

1

2

3

4

5

3lick vom Dach des Kaufhauses Kastner & Öhler auf den Schloßberg. **A view from the Kastner & Öhler department store towards Schloß-rg.** | 2 Die Außenfassade des Kaufhauses. **The exterior facade of the department store.** | 3 Große K & Ö-Halle im Jugendstil. **The large nouveau hall of the K & Ö department store.** | 4 Die Halle des Hauptbahnhofs als Kunstwerk: Franz Koglers Illusionsräume. **The hall of main train station as an art work: Franz Kogler's illusory space.** | 5 Türme prägen die Dachlandschaft. **Towers characterise the roofscape.**

1

2

3

4

5

Blick in die Innenhöfe: A look into the inner courtyards: 1 Wintergarten und Café des Hotels „Erzherzog Johann". The winter garden and café of the 'Erzherzog Johann' Hotel. | 2 Deutschritterordenshaus in der Sporgasse. The House of the Order of the Teutonic Knights in Sporgasse. | 3 Gastgarten des Gasthofs „Krebsenkeller". The outdoor dining area of the 'Krebsenkeller' restaurant. | 4 Palais Attems. Palais Attems. | 5 Palais Herberstein. Palais Herberstein.

Auf dem Schloßberg: **On Schloßberg:** | 1 Zifferblatt der Uhrturmuhr mit „vertauschten" Uhrzeigern. **The dials on the Clock Tower with 'inverted' hands.** | 2 Der Hackher-Löwe. **The Hackher Lion.** | 3 Uhrturm vom Herbersteingarten aus gesehen. **The Clock Tow seen from Herberstein garden.** | 4 Der Schloßbergsteig (Kriegssteig). **The Schloßberg steps (the war steps).**

4

1

2

3

1,2,3 Die Gastgärten auf dem Schloßberg haben zu jeder Jahreszeit Saison. **The outdoor dining areas of Schloßberg restaurants are in demand in all seasons.** | 4 1588 wurde die „Liesl" erbaut, der Glockenturm der alten Festung. **‚Liesl', the bell tower of the old fortifications was built in 1588.**

4

1 In den Schloßberg-Kasematten. **In the Schloßberg casemates.** | 2 Auf der Terrasse des Schloßbergrestaurants. **On the terrace of the Schloßberg Restaurant.** | 3 Nächtliches Lichtermeer vom Uhrturm aus. **A sea of light seen from the Clock Tower.** | 4 Schloßberglift. **The Schloßberg lift.** | 5 Wie praktisch – der Schloßberglift endet neben dem Café beim Uhrturm. **How convenient - the Schloßberg lift stops right next to the café near the Clock Tower.**

3

4

5

1

2

3

1,3 Viele Wege führen auf den Schloßberg. **Many paths lead to the top of Schloßberg.** | 2 Denkmal für Ludwig von Welden, der den Schloßberg zum Park umbaute. **A monument of Ludwig von Welden who converted Schloßberg into a park.** | 3 Die Stall- oder Kanonenbastei aus dem Jahr 1544. **The stable or cannon bastion dated 1544.**
4 Mit 60 Prozent Steigung fährt die Schloßbergbahn bergauf. **The Schloßbergbahn ascends a 60 degree gradient.**

•ie Kunst-Insel des New Yorkers Vito Acconci in der Mur ist eine Erinnerung an das Kulturhauptstadtjahr 2003 und verbindet die beiden 'fer des Flusses durch Metallstege. **The art-island in the River Mur by the New Yorker Vito Acconci is a memento of the Cultural apital Year 2003 and links both river banks by metal footbridges.**

1 Der Mariahilferplatz mit einem temporären Kunstobjekt im Rahmen des „Lendwirbels". **Mariahilferplatz with a temporary work of art during the local festival 'Lendwirbel'.** | 2 Bauernmarkt auf dem Lendplatz. **'The farmers' market on Lendplatz.** | 3 Buntes Leben in der Mariahilferstraße – direkt hinter dem Kunsthaus. **Colourful life on Mariahilferstraße – directly behind the Kunsthaus.**

2

3

Chikaku
Chikaku

Wie ein UFO liegt die „Blaue Blase“ des Kunsthauses am Murufer. **The ‘Blue Bubble’ sits next to the River Mur like an UFO.**

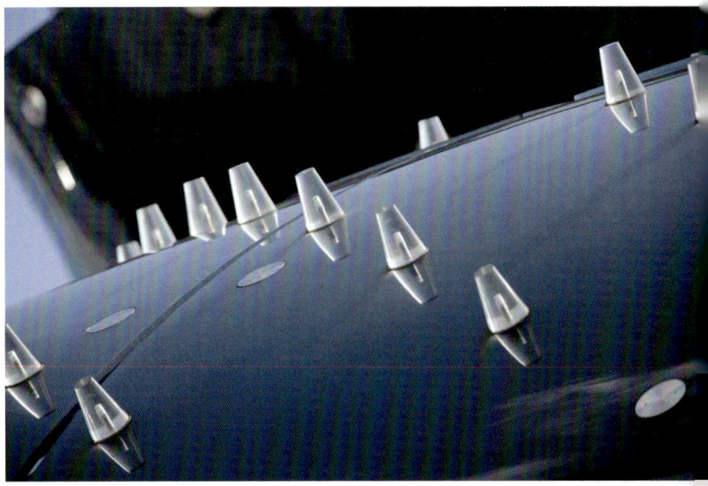

Das Kunsthaus von Peter Cook und Colin Fournier zieht seit dem Kulturhauptstadtjahr 2003 alle Blicke auf sich. **The Kunsthaus by Peter Cook and Colin Fournier has been drawing attention since the Cultural Capital Year 2003.**

1 Alt und Neu in gespiegelter Brechung: Kunst am Kunsthaus. **Old and new in a optical refraction: art on the Kunsthaus.** | 2 Auch ein Café darf im Museum nicht fehlen. **A museum is not complete without a café.** | 3 „Friendly Alien" haben die Architekten die „Blaue Blase" auch genannt. **The architects called the 'Blue Bubble' also 'Friendly Alien'.**

3

1

2

3

4

Schlösser der Liebe zieren das Geländer der Erzherzog-Johann-Brücke. **Padlocks of love adorn the railings of Erzherzog-Johann-Bridge.**
Ein Sandstrand an der Mur – auch das ist möglich. **A sandy beach on the River Mur – even that is possible.** | 3 Künstliche Wellen
ken Kanuten in die Mur. **Artificial waves draw canoeists to the River Mur.** | 4 Südtiroler Platz mit Eisernem Haus und Kunsthaus.
dtiroler Platz with the Eiserne Haus (Iron House) and the Kunsthaus.**

1

2

3

Der Türke im Palais Saurau. **The Turk in Palais Saurau.** | 2 Ein Bummel durch die Sporgasse. **A stroll through Sporgasse.**
Blick vom Schloßberg auf die alte Murvorstadt. **A view from Schloßberg over the old 'River Mur' suburb.**

SCHUBERT
SCHUBERT

Glöckl Bräu
Glöckl Bräu
Glöckl Bräu

n „Bermudadreieck": Viele Restaurants und Lokale zwischen Schubertkino, Glockenspielplatz und Mehlplatz verführen zur gemütlichen inkehr. **In the ‚Bermuda Triangle': Numerous restaurants and pubs between Schubertkino, Glockenspielplatz and Mehlplatz invite ne to linger.**

1

Eine anderer „Uhrturm" steht am Glockenspielplatz. **A different kind of 'Clock Tower' on Glockenspielplatz.** | 2 Der mächtige Innenhof des Priesterseminars. **The impressive courtyard of the Theological College.** | 3 La Strada-Aufführung. **La Strada performance.**

1 Die Stadtkrone – mit kaiserlichem Mausoleum, Dom, Schauspielhaus, Burg, Priesterseminar und Alter Universität. **The City Crown – with the Imperial Mausoleum, Cathedral, Theatre, Burg (castle), Theological College and Old University.** | 2 Engelfigur auf dem Mausoleum. **The figure of an angel on the Mausoleum.**

1

Spätgotisches Netzrippengewölbe im Dom. **A late Gothic ribbed vault in the Cathedral.** | 2 Der heilige Christophorus auf einer ıssade. **St. Christopher on a facade.** | 3 Heiliger Fürbitter. **A holy intercessor.** | 4 Blick auf die Kuppellandschaft von Mausoleum ıd Dom. **A view of the domes of the Mausoleum and Cathedral.**

as Mausoleum für Kaiser Ferdinand II. wurde ab 1614 von Giovanni Pietro de Pomis erbaut. **Giovanni Pietro de Pomis started building e Mausoleum of Emperor Ferdinand II. in 1614.**

1 Die Aula der Alten Universität als Tagungszentrum. **The auditorium of the Old University used as a congress centre.**

2 Schauspielhaus – vom Freiheitsplatz aus gesehen. **The Theatre seen from Freiheitsplatz.**

Café - Bar im Schauspielhaus
elenors
www.elenors.at
EBENE 3
Freiheitsplatz
2

1 Eingangstor in die Grazer Burg. **The entrance gate of the Grazer Burg (castle).** | 2 Gastgarten in der Hofgasse. **An outdoor dining area in Hofgasse.** | 3 Gotische Doppelwendeltreppe von Kaiser Maximilian I. in der Burg. **The Gothic double-spiral staircase installe in the Burg by Emperor Maximilian I.** | 4 Burggarten mit Blick auf den Kampanile des Mausoleums. **The Burg garden with a view over the Mausoleum campanile.**

4

1, 2 Orangerie im Burggarten. **The orangery in the Burg garden.** | 3 Hofbäckerei Edegger-Tax in der Hofgasse, eine der ältesten Bäckereien der Stadt. **Hofbäckerei Edegger-Tax in Hofgasse, one of the oldest bakeries in town.** | 4 Karmeliterplatz mit Wasserbecken und Pestsäule. **Karmeliterplatz with a water basin and plague column.**

4

Szenen der Ruhe und Erholung im Stadtpark. Scenes of peace and relaxation in the City Park.

1, 2 Opernredoute und Opernaufführung im Opernhaus. **The Opera Ball and opera performance in the Opera House.**

4 Nordansicht des 1898/99 erbauten Opernhauses. **A view of the northern facade of the Opera House built in 1898/99.**

3

1

2

3

4

5

6

Helmut-List-Halle. **Helmut List Hall.** | 2, 3 Stardirigent Nikolaus Harnoncourt, Konzertaufführung. **The star conductor Nikolaus arnoncourt, a concert.** | 4, 5 Stadthalle auf dem Messegelände. **Stadthalle on the trade-fair grounds.** 6 Creative Industries Con-ntion. **Creative Industries Convention.**

1 Karl-Franzens-Universität. The Karl-Franzens-University. | 2 Theologische Fakultät. The Faculty of Theology.
3 Das MUMUTH – Haus für Musik und Musiktheater an der KUG (Kunst Uni Graz). MUMUTH - the House of Music and Music Drama of KUG. | 4 Resowi-Zentrum der Universität. The Law and Social Science Centre of the University.

3

4

1 Die Gewächshäuser des Botanischen Instituts. **The greenhouses of the Institute of Botany.** | 2 Naherholungsgebiet Hilmteich. **A local recreational area Hilmteich.** | 3 Basilika Mariatrost, eine der größten Barockkirchen der Steiermark. **Mariatrost Basilica, one of Styria's largest baroque churches.**

1

1 Herz-Jesu-Kirche mit dem höchsten Kirchturm des Landes. Herz-Jesu-Kirche with the highest church steeple in the province. | 2 Die 1999 neu errichtete Synagoge in der Zweiglgasse. The synagogue in Zweiglgasse, newly constructed in 1999. | 3 Die frühgotische Leechkirche. The early Gothic Leechkirche.

Graz versinkt in der Abenddämmerung – nur Uhrturm, Mausoleum, Glockenturm „Liesl" und Herz-Jesu-Kirche stehen noch im Scheinwerferlicht.

Graz gradually disappears as dusk falls - only the Clock Tower, Mausoleum, Bell Tower 'Liesl' and Herz-Jesu-Kirche are still illuminated.

1

2

2 Seit 2010 Weltkulturerbe der UNESCO: das Barockschloss Eggenberg. **UNESCO World Heritage since 2010: the Baroque ggenberg Castle.** | 3–5 Prunkräume. **State Rooms.** | 3 Die Raunacher Räume. **The Raunacher Rooms.** | 4 Das Porzellanzimmer. **The Porcelain Room.** | 5 Der Planetensaal. **The Planetary Room.**

Graz im historischen Überblick

4000 v. Chr. Früheste Besiedlung auf dem Schloßberg und am heutigen Karmeliterplatz.

Seit dem 2. Jahrhundert v. Chr. Teil des keltischen Königreiches Noricum.

15. v. Chr. bis 476 n. Chr. Gehört das Gebiet zum Römischen Reich, das Grazer Feld ist eine dicht besiedelte Agrarlandschaft. Von einer am Westrand des Grazer Beckens verlaufenden Römerstraße zweigt ein Weg nach Osten ab, der die Mur über eine Furt bei der heutigen Erzherzog-Johann-Brücke überquert und entlang der Sporgasse über das alte Siedlungsgebiet am Karmeliterplatz Richtung Ungarn führt.

Im 6. Jahrhundert wandern nach Völkerwanderungszeit, Hunnensturm und Untergang des Weströmischen Reiches slawische Stämme in das verödete Gebiet und errichten auf dem Schloßberg eine kleine Burg (slaw. Gradec), von der sich der Name Graz ableitet.

Ende des 8. Jahrhunderts schlägt Karl der Große die Awaren, die bayrische Besiedlung des Raumes beginnt.

955 besiegt Kaiser Otto I. auf dem Lechfeld die Ungarn, die wieder nach Osten zurückgedrängt werden. Zur Sicherung des Heiligen Römischen Reiches Deutscher Nation entsteht ein Markengürtel vor den Ostalpen. Die Karantanische Mark wird zur Keimzelle der Steiermark.

1128 Erste Erwähnung von Graz in einer Urkunde des Klosters Rein, neueste Forschungen datieren eine erste Erwähnung bereits auf 1091.

Um 1160 übernimmt der Traungauer Markgraf Otakar III. von Steyr das Grazer Gebiet.

1164 erste Nennung eines Marktes hier, Graz entwickelt sich zur Landeshauptstadt.

1180 wird die Steiermark von Kaiser Friedrich Barbarossa zum Herzogtum erhoben und von Bayern unabhängig.

1240/45 erhält Graz den Panther des steirischen Herzogs als Stadtwappen – allerdings mit roten Flammenzungen, die aus allen Körperöffnungen kommen.

1379 Nach der Teilung des Habsburgerreiches im Vertrag von Neuberg wird Graz zur Residenz der Leopoldinischen Linie und damit zum Zentrum von Innerösterreich, das aus Steiermark, Kärnten, Triest, Görz, Inneristrien und Krain besteht.

1435 bis 1493 erlebt Graz seine erste Blüte: Herzog Friedrich V. (ab 1440 als Friedrich III. deutscher König, ab 1452 römischer Kaiser) macht die Stadt zu seiner bevorzugten Residenz, errichtet eine Stadtburg und lässt die alte Pfarrkirche Zum heiligen Ägydius im gotischen Stil neu errichten (heute Dom).

1439 und 1495 Vertreibung der Juden.

1480 Türken, Pest und Heuschrecken suchen den Grazer Raum heim („Landplagenbild" auf der Außenseite des Doms).

1499 Kaiser Maximilian I., Friedrichs Sohn, lässt in der Burg eine gotische Doppelwendeltreppe errichten.

1527 bis 1531 Das Landhaus in der Herrengasse wird als erster Renaissancebau der Stadt nach Plänen von Domenico dell'Allio erbaut und ist Sitz der Landstände.

Ab 1544 lässt Kaiser Ferdinand I. Graz von Domenico dell›Allio zur Hauptfestung Innerösterreichs ausbauen.

1564 bis 1619 zweite Blütezeit der Stadt: Graz wird Erzherzog Karls Residenzstadt von Innerösterreich, die Stadtkrone entsteht mit dem Ausbau von Burg, Dom, Jesuitenkolleg und Alter Universität.

1570 Errichtung der evangelischen Stiftskirche und Stiftsschule (heute Paradeishof), in der auch Johannes Kepler von 1594 bis 1600 unterrichtet.

1572 Berufung der Jesuiten nach Graz, die Rekatholisierung beginnt.

1600 Ausweisung aller evangelischen Bürger.

1619 Der Grazer Erzherzog Ferdinand von Innerösterreich wird zum römischen Kaiser gewählt und zieht als Ferdinand II. mit seinem Hof nach Wien.

1642 Antonio Solar erbaut das Landeszeughaus.

1664 Nach dem Sieg über die Türken vor Wien verliert Graz seine Bedeutung als Zentrum der Verteidigung.

1673 Kaiser Leopold I. vermählt sich in Graz mit Erzherzogin Claudia Felicitas von Tirol.

1773 Der Jesuitenorden wird vom Papst aufgelöst, die Grazer (Jesuiten-)Universität vom Staat übernommen.

1782 Kaiser Josef II. verfügt die Auflösung der alten Stadtbefestigung.

1786 Graz wird Bischofssitz.

1797 Die französische Revolutionsarmee Napoleons rückt in Graz ein.

1809 Nach erfolgloser dreiwöchiger Belagerung des Schloßbergs verlangt Napoleon im Friedensvertrag von Schönbrunn die Schleifung der Grazer Festung. Nur der Uhrturm und der Glockenturm „Liesl" bleiben für ein hohes Lösegeld der Bürger erhalten.

1811 Erzherzog Johann gründet mit seinen privaten Sammlungen das Joanneum.

19. Jahrhundert Graz wird zur Gartenstadt, der Schloßberg zur öffentlichen Parkanlage, das alte Glacis, also das freie Schussfeld vor der Stadtmauer, wird 1868 zum Stadtpark. Volksgarten und Augarten entstehen, Hilmteich und Leechwald werden von der Stadt erworben. Universitäten, Rathaus, Opernhaus und andere Prestigebauten werden errichtet.

1899 Eine elektrische Straßenbahn ersetzt die Pferdebahn.

1919 Nach dem Ersten Weltkrieg verliert Graz sein untersteirisches Hinterland im Süden und gerät in eine Randlage.

1938 Durch Eingemeindung der Nachbargemeinden wächst die Stadt von sechs auf 16 (heute 17) Bezirke.

1944/45 Schwere Luftangriffe werden durch die Alliierten auf Graz geflogen: 36 Prozent aller Gebäude werden beschädigt, fast 2000 Menschen sterben.

April 1945 Sowjetische Truppen besetzen Graz und werden im Juli von den Engländern abgelöst, die Zeit des Wiederaufbaus beginnt.

1960 Gründung des „Forum Stadtpark", Aufstieg von Graz zu einem Zentrum der künstlerischen Avantgarde im deutschen Sprachraum.

1968 Erster „steirischer herbst".

1974 Die Aktion „Rettet die Grazer Altstadt" verhindert eine Tiefgarage unter dem Landhaushof und führt zum Beschluss des Grazer Altstadterhaltungsgesetzes. Seit 1972 gibt es in der Herrengasse eine Fußgängerzone, die nun Zug um Zug erweitert wird.

1978 850-Jahrfeier der Stadt.

1999 Die Grazer Altstadt wird in die Liste des UNESCO-Weltkulturerbes aufgenommen.

2001 Graz wird zur ersten Menschenrechtsstadt Europas.

2003 Graz ist Kulturhauptstadt Europas.

2010 Schloss Eggenberg wird UNESCO-Weltkulturerbe.

März 2011 Graz wird „UNESCO City of Design".

November 2011 Das neue Joanneumsviertel mit dem Universalmuseum wird zur 200-Jahrfeier der Joanneumsgründung eröffnet.

Sommer 2012 Die Stadt Graz beginnt mit privaten Investoren auf den 54 Hektar großen Reininghaus gründen ein völlig neues Stadtviertel zu errichten.

2013 Eröffnung des Naturkundemuseums im Joanneumsviertel.

2014 Westlich des Hauptbahnhofs entsteht mit dem Namen „Smart City Project Graz Mitte" ein energieoptimierter Stadtteil, dessen Pilotprojekt bis 2017 umgesetzt sein soll.

Graz, a historical overview

4000 BC: the earliest settlement on Schloßberg and on today's Karmeliterplatz.

Since the 2nd century BC: part of the Celtic kingdom Noricum.

15 BC to 476 AD: the region forms part of the Roman Empire; the Graz Basin is a densely populated agricultural area. A path which branches off the Roman road leading along the western side of the Graz Basin, crosses the River Mur at a ford near today's Erzherzog-Johann-Bridge and then continues along Sporgasse across Karmeliterplatz in the direction of Hungary.

In the 6th century: after the time of the great migrations, the Hun invasion and the downfall of the Western Roman Empire, Slavic tribes migrate into the desolate area and build a small castle on Schloßberg (slav. Gradec), which the name Graz stems from.

At the end of the 8th century: Charlemagne beats the Avars; the Bavarian colonisation of the area starts.

955: Emperor Otto I beats the Hungarians on Lechfeld pushing them back towards the east. In order to safeguard the Holy Roman Empire of the German Nation, a belt of marches is created in front of the Eastern Alps. The Carantanian March becomes the nucleus of Styria.

1128: Graz is mentioned for the first time in a document of Rein Monastery. However, recent research indicates the first mention as early as 1091.

Around 1160: Traungau Margrave Otakar III. of Steyr takes over the area of Graz.

1164: a market is mentioned for the first time in this location; Graz develops into a regional capital.

1180: Emperor Friedrich Barbarossa elevates Styria to a duchy and makes it independent from Bavaria.

1240/45: Graz is awarded the Panther of the Styrian Duke as its municipal coats of arms. However, with red tongues of flames emanating from all orifices.

1379: after the Habsburg Empire is split up at the Treaty of Neuberg, Graz becomes the residence of the Leopoldinian line and, as that, the centre of Inner Austria which consists of Styria, Carinthia, Trieste, Gorizia, Inner Istria and Carniola.

1435 to 1493: Graz experiences its first heyday; Duke Friedrich V. (from 1440 German King as Friedrich III., from 1452 Holy Roman Emperor) makes the town his preferred residence, builds a town castle and re-builds the old parish church 'Zum heiligen Ägydius' [St. Giles] in Gothic style (today, the Cathedral).

1439 and 1495: the expulsion of the Jews.

1480: the Turks, the Black Death and locusts beset the area of Graz (picture of the 'Scourge' on the exterior of the Cathedral).

1499: Emperor Maximilian I., son of Friedrich, installs a Gothic double-spiral staircase in the castle.

1527 to 1531: the 'Landhaus' in Herrengasse is built as the first Renaissance building in Graz according to plans from Domenico dell'Allio and becomes the principal seat of the Styrian States.

From 1544 onwards: Emperor Ferdinand I. instructs Domenico dell'Allio to extend Graz to become the main fortress of Inner Austria.

1564 to 1619: the second heyday of the town; Graz becomes the Inner Austrian town of residence of Archduke Karl; the 'City Crown' is extended by enlarging the Castle, the Cathedral, the Jesuit College and the Old University.

1570: a Protestant monastery church and school are built (today's Paradeishof), where Johannes Kepler taught from 1594 to 1600.

1572: the Jesuits are called to Graz, the re-Catholisation begins.

1600: the expulsion of all Protestant citizens starts.

1619: the Archduke of Graz, Ferdinand of Inner Austria is elected Holy Roman Emperor and moves his court to Vienna as Ferdinand II.

1642: Antonio Solar builds the State Armoury.

1664: after the Turks are conquered at Vienna, Graz loses importance as a centre of defence.

1673: Emperor Leopold I marries Archduchess Claudia Felicitas of Tyrol in Graz.

1773: the Order of the Jesuits is dissolved by the Pope and the State takes over Graz (Jesuit) University.

1782: Emperor Josef II gives instructions for the old city fortification to be dismantled.

1786: Graz becomes an episcopal see.

1797: the French Revolutionary Army of Napoleon enters Graz.

1809: after an unsuccessful, three week long siege of Schlossberg, Napoleon demands the destruction of the fortress of Graz to be included in the Treaty of Schönbrunn. Only after the citizens pay a high ransom, the Clock Tower and the bell tower 'Liesl' are left standing.

1811: Archduke Johann founds the Joanneum with his private collections.

19th century: Graz becomes a city of gardens, the Schloßberg is converted into a public park, the old Glacis, i.e., the field of fire outside the city walls, becomes the City Park in 1868: The Volksgarten and Augarten parks are created; the city acquires the Hilmteich (pond at the outskirts of Graz) and the Leech Forest. Universities, the Town Hall, the Opera House and other prestigious buildings are constructed.

1899: the horse-drawn tram is substituted by an electric tram.

1919: after the First World War, Graz loses its Lower Styrian hinterland in the south and becomes a marginalised region.

1938: through the integration of several neighbouring municipalities, the city grows in size from 6 to 16 (today 17) districts.

1944/45: Allied Forces carry out heavy air raids over Graz; 36 percent of all buildings are damaged, nearly 2,000 people die.

April 1945: Soviet troops occupy Graz and are relieved by the British in July; a time of reconstruction begins.

1960: 'Forum Stadtpark' is founded. Graz becomes the centre of avant-garde art in the German-speaking area.

1968: first 'steirischer herbst (Styrian Autumn).

1974: the protest action 'Save the Old Town of Graz' stops an underground car park from being built under the Landhaushof and leads to the creation of the Old Town Preservation Law. Herrengasse becomes a pedestrian zone in 1972 and is gradually expanded.

1978: the city celebrates its 850th anniversary.

1999: the Old Town of Graz is included in the 'UNESCO World Heritage' list.

2001: Graz becomes Europe's first 'City of Human Rights'.

2003: Graz becomes Europe's 'Capital of Culture'.

2010: Eggenberg Castel is nominated as a 'UNESCO World Heritage' site.

March 2011: Graz becomes 'UNESCO City of Design'.

November 2011: the new Joanneum Quarter with the Universal Museum is opened on the occasion of the 200th anniversary of the foundation of Joanneum.

Summer 2012: With private investors, the city of Graz begins to build a totally new suburb on the 54-hectare Reininghaus grounds.

2013: opening of the Museum of Natural History in the Joanneum Quarter.

2014: West of the main train station, an energy-optimised district with the name "Smart City Project Graz Mitte" will begin construction, the pilot project of which is supposed to be implemented by 2017.

Der Fotograf

Harry Schiffer, geboren 1967 in Graz, offizieller Fotograf der Kulturhauptstadt Graz 2003, Fotos für div. Magazine, Tourismusfotos in Wien, Kärnten, Burgenland, Südtirol und Steiermark. Ausgedehnte Fotoreisen rund um die Welt, verschiedene Ausstellungen im In- und Ausland.
Harry Schiffer hat seine Leidenschaft zum Beruf gemacht. Seine Lieblingsmotive sind Graz und die Steiermark, Als offizieller Fotograf von „Steiermark Tourismus" und „Graz Tourismus" ist er ein besonderer Kenner von Graz und der Steiermark und ihrer Gustostückerln.

Aboput the photographer

**Harry Schiffer; born 1967 in Graz; in 2003 official photographer of Capital of Culture Graz 2003; photos for various magazines, tourism photos in Vienna, Carinthia, Burgenland, Southern Tyrol and Styria. Extensive photographic journeys around the world, various exhibitions in Austria and abroad.
Harry Schiffer has turned his passion into his profession with his favourite motives being Graz and Styria. As the official photographer for Steiermark Tourismus and Graz Tourismus, he knows Graz and Styria and their highlights particularly well.**

Der Autor

Robert Engele, geboren 1949 in Graz, studierte Germanistik und Anglistik in Graz und Oxford. Von 1976 bis 1978 Deutsch-Lektor im Gonville & Caius College in Cambridge, danach zwei Jahre beim „steirischen herbst". Ab 1980 Verlagslektor, seit 2003 Redakteur bei der „Kleinen Zeitung". Zuletzt von ihm im Styria Verlag erschienen: „Graz. Eine Stadt in Bildern", „Kramasuri", „Damals in Graz" und „Damals in der Steiermark".

About the author

**Robert Engele, born in Graz in 1949. Studied German and English Studies in Graz and Oxford. German lecturer at the Gonville & Caius College in Cambridge, then worked for the "steirischer herbst" in Graz. In 1980 editor an since 2003 journalist for the "Kleine Zeitung".
Most recently published by him by Styria Verlag "Graz. Eine Stadt in Bildern", "Kramasuri", "Damals in Graz" and "Damals in der Steiermark".**

ISBN 978-3-7012-0199-0
styria verlag

7 6 5 4 3 2

Bücher aus der Verlagsgruppe Styria
gibt es in jeder Buchhandlung
und im Onlineshop
www.styriabooks.at

Übersetzung: Lanquagepoint/
V. + P. Kostan
Lektorat: Christine Wiesenhofer
Umschlaggestaltung: Maria Schuster
Buchgestaltung: Andrea Malek,
malanda-Buchdesign.at, Graz
Druck und Bindung: Neografia
Printed in EU

Seite 5, rechts: Kunsthaus mit Turm der Franziskanerkirche. **Kunsthaus with church spire of the Franziskanerkirche.**

Seite 6: Herrengasse. **Herrengasse.**

Seite 7, links: Dachterrasse des Kaufhauses Kastner & Öhler. **Roof-deck of the Kastner & Öhler department store.**

Seite 8: Hauptplatz mit Erzherzog-Johann-Denkmal. **The Main Square with the monument of Archduke Johann.**

Seite 12: Johannes Kepler. **Johannes Kepler.**

Seite 13: Hotel Erzherzog Johann – Wintergarten. **Hotel Erzherzog Johann - Winter garden.**

Seite 15: Schloss Eggenberg. **Schloss Eggenberg.**

Seite 16: Landeszeughaus – der Steirische Panther. **Styrian Armoury - the Styrian Panther.**

Seite 20: Joanneum Museumsviertel. **Joanneum Quarter.**